LAOS

...in Pictures

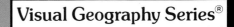

Visual Geography Series®

LAOS

...in Pictures

Prepared by
Geography Department

Lerner Publications Company
Minneapolis

Photo © Andrew E. Beswick

**A Laotian worker repairs one of Laos's many Buddhist
temples.**

This book is a newly commissioned title in the Visual
Geography Series. The text is set in 10/12 Century
Textbook.

LIBRARY OF CONGRESS CATALOGING-IN-PUBLICATION DATA

Laos in pictures / prepared by Geography Department,
    Lerner Publications Company.
    p. cm.—(Visual Geography Series)
    Includes index.
    Summary: Introduces the land, history, government,
people and economy of the only country in Southeast Asia
that has no seacoast.
    ISBN 0–8225–1906–2 (lib. bdg.: alk. paper)
    1. Laos—Juvenile literature. [1 Laos.] I. Lerner Pub-
lications Company. Geography Dept. II. Series: Visual
geography series (Minneapolis, Minn.)
DS555.3.L345   1996
959.4—dc20   95–37182

International Standard Book Number: 0–8225–1906–2
Library of Congress Catalog Card Number: 95–37182

VISUAL GEOGRAPHY SERIES®

Publisher
Harry Jonas Lerner
Senior Editor
Mary M. Rodgers
Editor
Lori Ann Coleman
Joan Freese
Colleen Sexton
Photo Researcher
Beth Johnson
Consultants/Contributors
David Wright
Douglas Pike
Sandra K. Davis
Designer
Jim Simondet
Cartographer
Carol F. Barrett
Indexer
Sylvia Timian
Production Manager
Gary J. Hansen

Photo © Andrew E. Beswick

**Water buffalo munch grass in front of a typical Laotian
dwelling.**

Acknowledgments

Title page photo © Nevada Wier.

Elevation contours adapted from *The Times Atlas of
the World,* seventh comprehensive edition (New York:
Times Books, 1985).

1 2 3 4 5 6 – JR – 01 00 99 98 97 96

Uniformed secondary-level students welcome a foreign visitor to their school. Since the late 1980s, when the Laotian government became less restrictive, more outsiders have been allowed into Laos.

Contents

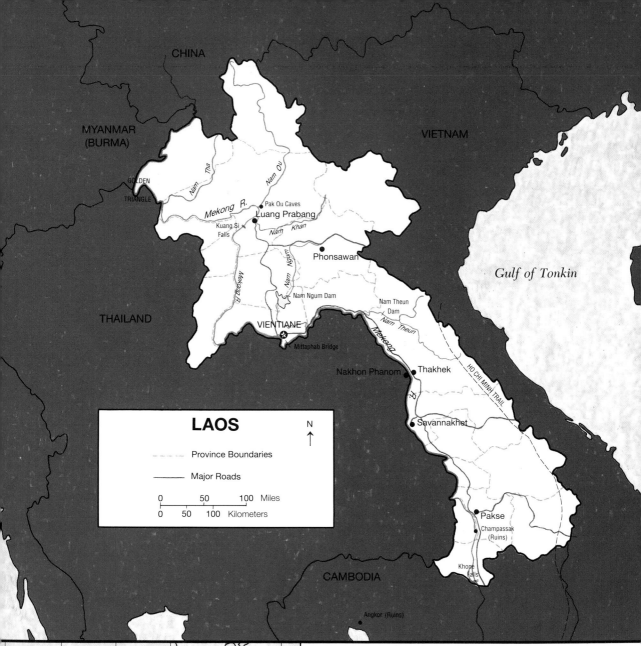

CHINA

MYANMAR
(BURMA)

VIETNAM

GOLDEN
TRIANGLE

Nam Tha

Nam Ou

Mekong R.

Pak Ou Caves
Luang Prabang

Kuang Si
Falls

Nam Khan

Mekong R.

Nam Ngum

Phonsawan

THAILAND

Nam Ngum Dam

Nam Theun
Dam

Nam Theun

VIENTIANE

Mittaphab Bridge

Mekong R.

Nakhon Phanom • Thakhek

HO CHI MINH TRAIL

Gulf of Tonkin

LAOS

N
↑

- - - Province Boundaries

——— Major Roads

| 0 | 50 | 100 | Miles |
| 0 | 50 | 100 | Kilometers |

Savannakhet

Pakse
Champassak
(Ruins)

Khone
Falls

CAMBODIA

Angkor (Ruins)

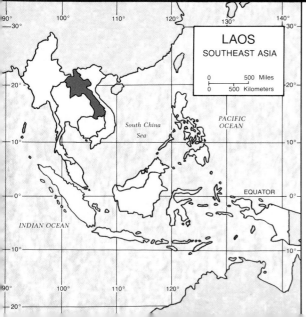

90° 100° 110° 120° 130° 140°

30° 30°

LAOS
SOUTHEAST ASIA

| 0 | 500 | Miles |
| 0 | 500 | Kilometers |

20° 20°

*South China
Sea*

*PACIFIC
OCEAN*

10° 10°

0° 0°

EQUATOR

INDIAN OCEAN

10° 10°

90° 100° 110° 120°

20°

METRIC CONVERSION CHART
To Find Approximate Equivalents

WHEN YOU KNOW:	MULTIPLY BY:	TO FIND:
AREA		
acres	0.41	hectares
square miles	2.59	square kilometers
CAPACITY		
gallons	3.79	liters
LENGTH		
feet	30.48	centimeters
yards	0.91	meters
miles	1.61	kilometers
MASS (weight)		
pounds	0.45	kilograms
tons	0.91	metric tons
VOLUME		
cubic yards	0.77	cubic meters
TEMPERATURE		
degrees Fahrenheit	0.56 (*after* subtracting 32)	degrees Celsius

Figures in golden relief decorate the exterior of Wat Xieng Thong, a temple in the former Laotian capital of Luang Prabang. Some of the carvings at the 400-year-old site depict stories from the *Ramayana,* a Hindu epic that came to Laos with Indian traders and is the country's most important piece of literature.

Introduction

Laos is a landlocked, mountainous country in Southeast Asia. With a population of 4.8 million, Laos is the region's most thinly settled nation. Isolation and a sparse population have greatly impacted the country's long history as well as its modern social and economic situation. These characteristics also make Laos different from its neighbors whose geographic locations have allowed for greater contact with outsiders and for more intensive settlement.

Although humans have inhabited Laos for thousands of years, the country's recorded past begins in the fourteenth century. Historians believe the first inhabitants of the area lived in the highlands of northern Laos.

Later settlers came from China by following the Mekong River, a waterway that runs south from China through Laos, Cambodia, and Vietnam. Along the river, early Laotians farmed and hunted. For centuries traders and immigrants arrived in the region from India and China, introducing new political systems and religious faiths. Over the years, these newcomers intermarried with the original inhabitants of Laos, and a distinct Laotian nation gradually emerged.

The first Laotian states were small kingdoms. They arose in the fourteenth century and ruled central Laos from the historic capital of Luang Prabang. (The country's modern capital is Vientiane.) Despite occasional problems, these realms lasted for several hundred years.

Internal conflicts erupted at the start of the 1700s, when different members of the Laotian royal family sought support from their powerful neighbors in Burma (present-day Myanmar), Siam (modern Thailand), or Vietnam. These foreign governments divided and ruled the country until the late nineteenth century, when French explorers began moving up the Mekong River into Laos. By 1893 France was claiming much of Southeast Asia—including Laos, Cambodia, and Vietnam—as its colony. Collectively these countries became known as French Indochina.

During World War II (1939–1945), the Japanese swept across lower Asia, taking control of French Indochina. After the defeat of Japan in 1945, an independence movement strengthened in the Laotian countryside—as did parallel activities in Vietnam and Cambodia. Members of the Lao royal family rallied the Laotians against reimposed French control. In 1955 France officially recognized Laos as an independent nation.

But turmoil among Laos's many political factions worsened. One group, the royalists, supported a monarchy. Another favored a Communist government, in which the state controls and owns all industries, factories, and businesses.

After France granted Laos and the rest of French Indochina independence, a redistribution of power took place and brought warfare to much of Southeast Asia. Civil war broke out in Laos during the 1960s between the Communists, known as the Pathet Lao, and their enemies. At the same time, similar struggles were being fought in Vietnam and Cambodia.

In 1975 Pathet Lao forces captured Vientiane and formed a government that outlawed opposing political parties. At least 350,000 citizens have fled Laos since the Communist takeover. These people left their homeland to escape a system that denies most personal freedoms, including the rights to privacy, to free speech, to assemble, and to travel in and out of the country.

The regime's strict policies led to economic decline in the 1980s, and Laotian leaders adopted several important reforms to address the problems. By the 1990s, Laos was permitting new shops to open and allowing farmers to sell their goods privately. Although Laos has made these changes in economic policy, political and social reforms have been much slower to occur.

The country has maintained its single-party political system in which opposition parties are still illegal. Laos also remains overwhelmingly poor, and its citizens have little freedom to improve their situation. Whether a better life awaits the people of Laos remains to be seen as the nation continues to face an uncertain future.

A Laotian knife sharpener plies his trade on the street. The government now permits more small businesses to operate and to keep the profits from their work.

Water cascades down a rugged section of Laos's mountainous area, which covers more than two-thirds of the nation's land.

1) The Land

The only landlocked country in Southeast Asia, Laos lies in the middle of the Indochinese Peninsula—a long, narrow landform that also holds the nations of Vietnam, Cambodia, Thailand, and Myanmar. With a total land area of 91,428 square miles, Laos is slightly smaller than the state of Oregon.

Laos is bordered by China to the north, Vietnam to the east, and Cambodia to the south. Thailand lies west of Laos, and Myanmar sits to the northwest. Laos extends about 650 miles in length from the northwest to the southeast. The nation's widest point, in the north, is 290 miles from west to east. By contrast, parts of the southeastern panhandle—the thin, armlike projection of land that makes up the middle of the country—do not reach 100 miles in width.

Topography

Laos is mainly a mountainous nation, with limited level land. These characteristics make communication, transportation, and farming difficult and contribute to the Laotian people's isolation from one another and from greater Southeast Asia.

The mountains of Laos dominate the landscape, covering more than two-thirds of the country. In fact, more than 90 percent of the land rises to over 600 feet above sea level. Mount Phou Bia in north central Laos is the country's highest point, reaching an elevation of 9,248 feet.

In northern Laos, rugged mountains run from the northeast to the southwest and are separated by narrow valleys that hold dense rain-forests. Along Laos's eastern border with Vietnam, the rugged Annamese Cordillera (a mountain range called the Troung Son by the Vietnamese) blocks transportation. At the narrowest point of the Laotian panhandle, these mountains reach the valley of the Mekong

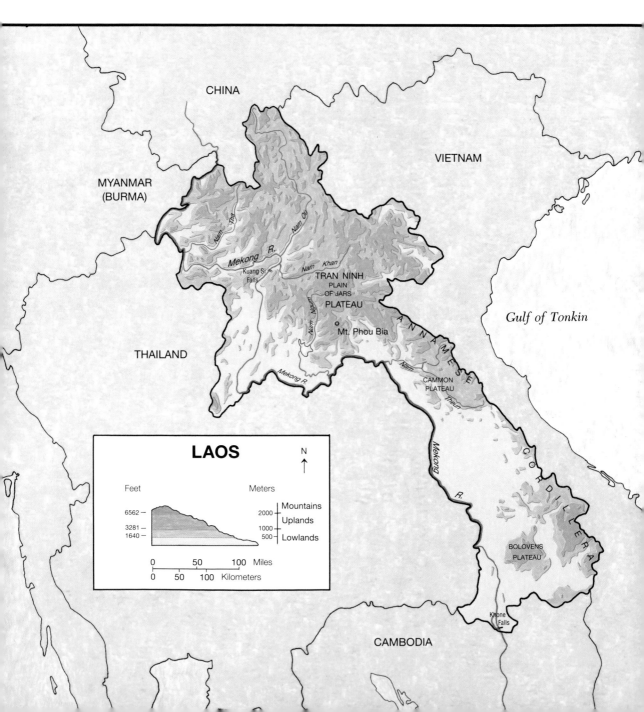

CHINA

MYANMAR (BURMA)

VIETNAM

Nam Tha

Nam Ou

Mekong R.

Nam Khan

Kuang Si Falls

TRAN NINH

PLAIN OF JARS

PLATEAU

Nam Ngum

Mt. Phou Bia

Gulf of Tonkin

THAILAND

A N N A M E S E

Mekong R.

Nam Theun

CAMMON PLATEAU

Mekong R.

C O R D I L L E R A

LAOS

N

Feet   Meters

6562 —   2000 — Mountains
3281 —   1000 — Uplands
1640 —   500 — Lowlands

0   50   100   Miles
0   50   100   Kilometers

BOLOVENS PLATEAU

Khone Falls

CAMBODIA

Kuang Si Falls, a spectacular waterfall in northern Laos that tumbles over limestone formations, ends in a series of small green pools surrounded by vegetation.

The wide Mekong River is one of Laos's main physical features. The use and control of the waterway have become issues of concern not only for Laos but for its Southeast Asian neighbors as well.

River, which forms much of Laos's western border. Limestone caves, steep rock formations, and sinkholes (hollow places in which rainwater collects) are common at the southern end of the Annamese chain.

A series of three plateaus runs from north to south through Laos. Northern Laos holds the Tran Ninh Plateau, which includes a rolling grassland known as the Plain of Jars, so named for the large ancient containers found there.

In central Laos, the Cammon Plateau reaches the foothills of the Annamese Cordillera. This region has karst—a type of limestone with sinkholes, underground streams, and caverns. At the southern end of Laos, near the border with Cambodia, is the Bolovens Plateau, a fertile and wooded plain surrounded by steep slopes. These plateaus, along with the floodplains of the Mekong River, comprise the only level land in Laos. They link the Mekong

11

Fishers use various methods to net their catch in the Mekong. One approach involves gathering and throwing a round net *(above)* while balancing on a small boat. Laotians also stand in the river *(below)*, sinking and raising nets on poles to collect the fish, which are then stored in baskets.

River Valley in the west with the highlands of the eastern border regions.

In Laos's lowland areas along the Mekong River, seasonal flooding leaves rich silt deposits. Intensively farmed, these lowlands boast the many irrigated rice paddies that provide much of the nation's staple food supply.

Rivers

The Mekong River, the principal waterway of Southeast Asia, flows for 2,600 miles from its source in the mountains of Tibet (called Xizang in China). From this remote area of China, the river churns between steep mountainsides and then passes through the Golden Triangle—the region where Laos, Myanmar, and Thailand meet. The Mekong forms much of Laos's western border before exiting the country at Khone Falls, 1,200 miles to the southeast. The river travels into Cambodia and then into the Mekong Delta of southern

Vietnam. Here the river empties into the South China Sea, an arm of the Pacific Ocean.

Large rocks make travel on the upper Mekong dangerous, especially during the dry season, when the river's water level is low. In the rainy summer months, the Mekong can swell to 40 feet above its banks and can extend to 14 miles in width. Steep falls and treacherous rapids hamper the passage of river craft during this season.

In certain seasons and in certain areas, the river nevertheless provides many Laotians with a useful transportation route. Riverboats carry crops and livestock to market and people from town to town. The Mekong also deposits hundreds of tons of fertile soil on the farmland and rice paddies of western Laos. In addition, the river supplies fish for lowland dwellers.

Other important rivers in Laos include the Nam Ou, the Nam Tha, and the Nam Ngum, all of which run westward into the Mekong River. The Nam Ngum powers a large hydroelectric station near Vientiane, the Laotian capital city. The Laotian government is planning to build several other big dams along the Mekong. Some Laotians fear that these projects, if developed improperly, could cause environmental problems.

Although most Laotian waterways empty into the Mekong, a few northern rivers flow eastward through Vietnam and into the Gulf of Tonkin, another arm of the South China Sea. These networks of smaller streams and canals also feed Laotian rice paddies, allowing some growers to raise two crops each year.

Climate

Laos is a warm, tropical country with three distinct seasons. A cool and dry period lasts from November to February. Hotter weather prevails from the middle of February to May, followed by a

Umbrellas protect Laotians from a monsoon shower (a seasonal downpour) as they travel up the Nam Khan, a river that flows into the Mekong near Luang Prabang.

A tropical storm streaks across the sky near Vientiane, the Laotian capital.

rainy season that lasts from May until October.

Two monsoons—seasonal rain-bearing winds—sweep across Southeast Asia each year and affect the Laotian climate. The northeast monsoon delivers little rain but is responsible for cool breezes from November to mid-February. The southwest monsoon, which comes in May or June, brings cloudy skies and heavy rains. As much as 160 inches of rain drenches the Bolovens Plateau in southern Laos, and at least 50 inches fall at many of the country's other elevations.

The rain comes in different forms in different areas. A very fine, dustlike moisture blows through the mountains, while brief but heavy downpours fall for weeks in the lowlands at about the same time every day. Violent storms known as typhoons roll westward from the Pacific Ocean and through the South China Sea but weaken as they move inland through Vietnam and Laos.

Temperatures vary a great deal from season to season and from place to place. High in the Annamese Cordillera, nighttime readings can drop below freezing from November into February. In the lowlands, spring temperatures exceed 90°F almost every day. Vientiane averages 70°F in winter, 89°F in spring, and 82°F during the rainy season.

Flora and Fauna

Laos is home to many types of plants and animals. A great variety of evergreen and deciduous (leaf-shedding) trees grows in the monsoon forests of southern Laos, where the climate is not wet enough for tropical rain-forests. Although loggers in Laos's tropical rain-forests are harvesting teak, mahogany, and other tropical hardwoods in increasing numbers, these rain-forests still thrive in the highlands of northern and eastern Laos. High rainfall and humidity support these complex ecosystems.

The country's woodlands are also threatened by farmers, who clear large acreages for cropland by felling trees and burning vegetation. This technique is known as slash-and-burn farming. The forests are just beginning to recover from damage that occurred in the 1960s and 1970s, the era of the Vietnam War, when chemical sprays and bombs caused considerable destruction throughout the region.

Despite the loss of some forest cover, Laos still has more safe, remote areas for animals than does any other nation in Southeast Asia. Once described as the land of a million elephants, Laos has tame as well as wild elephant herds. Many types of oxen, large cats, birds, fish, and reptiles live in heavily forested areas. Insects include stinging wasps, scorpions, and many kinds of beetles. At least 100 butterfly species flutter throughout the country, even during dry months.

Especially numerous are snakes, some of which are poisonous. At least half a dozen of the more than 100 varieties—including kraits, coral snakes, and pythons—are dangerous to humans. The king cobra, which may reach a length of

Photo © John Elk III

Water buffalo are common animals in Laos, where they help farmers plow and harvest their crops.

Some farmers in the hills of Laos use a land-clearing method called slash-and-burn that has depleted some of the nation's woodlands.

Photo by B. Moser/The Hutchison Library

18 feet, is the longest poisonous snake on earth. Even longer are nonpoisonous pythons, which can be 30 feet long.

Natural Resources

The extensive forests of Laos remain the nation's most profitable natural resource. The country's most common mineral of value is tin, which is mined extensively in the west central panhandle. Gypsum, a mineral used in making plaster, is also a major resource. Stocks of salt are mined on a small scale. The coal deposits of northern Laos are largely untouched because there is no way to transport them to processing centers. The country also has undeveloped stocks of gold, zinc, lead, and silver, as well as petroleum reserves.

Laos's numerous rivers make hydropower a potentially valuable energy resource. These rivers also yield more than 20,000 tons of fish each year. Fish species range from finger-sized types that are dried before being eaten to huge catfish that swim upriver in the Mekong.

Photo © Andrew E. Beswick

Although not a major resource, salt exists in large enough quantities to employ a small number of Laotian workers. Here, the laborers close the bags after the mineral has been gathered and dried.

Photo © Andrew E. Beswick

Wood from Laos's forests provides most of the cooking and heating fuel in the country's homes.

In Vientiane a vendor passes in front of the Lao Revolutionary Museum, which is housed in a mansion originally built by the French in the 1800s.

Cities

Only 19 percent of Laos's 4.8 million people are urban dwellers. Laotian cities feature two-story stucco buildings that serve as both shops and houses. Two-story brick structures, dating to the French-colonial period, also line some streets. Inexpensive and plentiful woods—such as palm and bamboo—and palm thatch are commonly used for housing, especially in less-developed areas. More costly homes are built with teak and other tropical hardwoods.

Typical Laotian homes are raised above ground and use thatch, bamboo, and other commonplace materials for their construction.

Photo © Nevada Wier

Vientiane's wide Lan Xang Street stretches from the Patuxai, a war memorial honoring pre-revolutionary heroes, to the presidential palace.

The nation's capital, Vientiane, is the largest city. Other populated areas include Savannakhet, Pakse, and the former capital, Luang Prabang. All four cities lie on the eastern bank of the Mekong River. Although they have grown steadily in the late twentieth century, these urban areas have yet to see many cars, buses, and trucks.

VIENTIANE

Compared to other capitals in Southeast Asia, Vientiane (population 377,409) is small and quiet, having survived the Vietnam War era untouched. The city features tree-lined boulevards, well-preserved temples, and many structures dating from the French-colonial period.

Located on the Mekong River in central Laos, Vientiane has existed for almost 1,000 years and has seen Burmese, Khmer (Cambodian), Siamese, and Vietnamese rulers. Throughout Laotian history, Vientiane vied with Luang Prabang as the capital city. In 1893, under French control, Vientiane became the permanent, modern capital. A few French-speaking residents still call the city home.

When the Communist Pathet Lao took control of Vientiane in 1975, they shut down most businesses—a move that prompted some residents to flee. After economic reforms began in the 1980s, Vientiane again benefited from its location on the busy Mekong. In recent years, small shops and other kinds of private enterprises have added some bustle to the city's streets. The country's leading commercial center, Vientiane boasts busy hotels, restaurants, and street markets, as well as a growing population. Some Laotians fear that increased development will overwhelm the city with new construction, urban crowding, and stiff competition for jobs.

SECONDARY CITIES

Savannakhet (population 96,652) also lies on the Mekong River, about 200 miles downriver from Vientiane. Savannakhet's small business district sits near a river dock, from which a ferry moves passengers and handmade Laotian ceramics across the Mekong to Thailand. The city features attractive European- and Asian-style buildings, as well as Buddhist temples and a Catholic church.

Since the late nineteenth century, when the French took over Indochina as a colony, Savannakhet has included a large Vietnamese community, whose inhabitants worked in civil service positions for the French government. The rest of the city's population is a mix of Khmer, Chinese, various Laotian ethnic minorities, and a small number of Europeans. Foreign travelers use Savannakhet as a jumping-off point for travel to the Ho Chi Minh Trail, a famous wartime supply route that passed in and out of Laos.

Luang Prabang, a well-preserved and historic city of 68,399 people, is about 100 miles north of Vientiane. Bicycles outnumber motor vehicles in Luang Prabang, where devout Buddhists can visit dozens of historic wats (temples) and other religious sites. The city became the seat of the Lao monarchy in A.D. 1353. It continued to be the home of members of the Lao royal family until 1975, when the Communist regime took power and ousted the last Laotian king.

Pakse (population 47,323) lies on the Mekong River, about 50 miles north of the Cambodian border, in one of the few areas where both banks of the Mekong belong to Laos. Less than a century old, the city was founded by the French in 1905. From Pakse boats and trucks carry lumber to markets in Thailand. Many Pakse residents are Chinese or Vietnamese.

An aerial view of Luang Prabang shows the former capital's broad streets, plentiful greenery, and imposing buildings. The seat of the Laotian monarchy until the 1500s, the city remained an important religious and political hub following the government's move to Vientiane.

Vendors gather outside a colonial-era house in Pakse. This small but thriving lowland town is the gateway to Champassak, an ancient religious site in Southeast Asia.

Sunset bathes the large stone containers on the Plain of Jars in a golden light. Historians speculate that this area became home to some of the earliest residents of the Indochinese Peninsula, which holds Laos, Vietnam, Cambodia, Thailand, and Myanmar.

2) History and Government

Although Laos has been inhabited for thousands of years, its recorded history begins only in the fourteenth century. Evidence of the people and rulers of earlier times exists in artifacts, in accounts written in other regions such as China, and in ancient legends passed on by the culture's storytellers.

First Settlers

Archaeologists believe that hunters and gatherers living north of the Plain of Jars were the first settlers on the Indochinese Peninsula. Taking advantage of the protection offered by caves, these peoples lived in the mountains rather than in the plains and river valleys. As their numbers grew, the people gradually moved to the Plain of Jars and other lowlands, where they kept herds of cattle and began raising rice and other grain crops.

By 2000 B.C., the early people of Laos were building settlements in the Mekong River Valley. Using bronze-making techniques, settlers created tools, weapons, and utensils. The people traded these useful items with other Southeast Asians and with the Chinese, who lived to the north. The making of iron began in the plains and valleys in about the fifth century B.C.

The early settlers eventually established small chiefdoms, known as *mandalas,* in the Mekong River Valley. Through trade in goods and food, these states came under the cultural influence of China and of India, a large territory to the west. At the same time, the rugged mountains and remote forests of Laos saw little Indian or Chinese settlement. Here the descendants of the earliest peoples had little contact with the lowlands and were well beyond the reach of the new civilizations. For hundreds of years, the inhabitants of Laos lived peacefully, farming and trading in the country's valleys and highlands.

Champa and Funan

By the late fifth century A.D., Indian settlers had founded Champa, a realm of small states stretching eastward from the central Mekong River Valley, through portions of present-day Vietnam, to the South China Sea. The administrative hub—Champassak—lay on the western bank of the Mekong, near Laos's modern borders with Thailand and Cambodia. Indian newcomers brought Sanskrit, a written language, and Hinduism, a religious system that emphasizes duty and individual destiny.

To the south of Champa was Funan, a rival state centered in what is now Cambodia and the Mekong Delta of southern Vietnam. Although the founders of Funan were Khmer (modern Cambodian) in origin, Funan also was heavily influenced by settlers from India. The chief city of Funan, called Vyadhapura, was not far from the present-day Cambodian capital of Phnom Penh. Champa and Funan competed for power in the region, but Funan had more success in the rivalry.

Late in the ninth century, in what is now northwestern Cambodia, the Khmer established Angkor as the capital of a powerful empire known as Kambuja. The people who populated this realm controlled Cambodia as well as southern and central

Photo © Nik Wheeler

The ruins of Champassak *(above)* sit near Laos's present-day western frontier. Originally the site of an Indian realm, the spot later was taken over by the Khmer (modern Cambodians) and made part of the Kambuja Empire. Statues still standing at Champassak *(below)* reflect Hindu and Buddhist influences.

Photo © Nik Wheeler

Laos. The building of elaborate stone temples at Angkor symbolized the power of the Khmer culture to neighboring kingdoms.

The Khmer gradually enlarged Kambuja, while monks from what is now Thailand spread the new faith of Theravada Buddhism to the central and upper Mekong. By the 1100s, the Khmer were occupying the area of Vientiane, which centuries before had been set up as a river-valley *muong* (district). As Khmer power expanded, the highland peoples of the north, called Kha (or slaves), came under Kambuja's control. But soon a new wave of migration from the north checked the expansion of the Khmer state.

Tai Migrations

The new immigration was the result of centuries of movement farther north. Beginning in the eighth century, ethnic Tai peoples of southern China and northern Vietnam had been traveling south from their empire of Nan Chao. Gradually, the

Tai arrived in central Laos and intermarried with the inhabitants of the area's forests and mountains. According to Laotian legend, a Tai prince founded the Luang Prabang principality (realm of a prince) at this time. He descended from Khoun Lo, the seventh son of a ruler of Nan Chao.

Historians in China and Vietnam gave a new name—Lao—to the small principalities built by the migrating Tai. (The ethnic Lao are a branch of the ethnic Tai people.) From China the Tai brought new methods of agriculture to Laos. The Tai cut away hillsides to create flat terraces on which crops could be grown. They also built canals and a system of irrigation to water large rice fields, a technique known as wet rice cultivation.

The Tai spread throughout Southeast Asia, setting up new principalities in Vietnam, Burma, Thailand, and as far west as India. But by the 1200s the Tai kingdom was under attack by Kublai Khan, a Mongol warlord from the plains of central Asia. In 1253 Kublai Khan destroyed Nan Chao,

Photo by Bettmann Archive

Khmer power reached its height beginning in the ninth century A.D., when Kambuja occupied southern and central Laos. Huge stone temples, called wats, rose in the capital city of Angkor, Cambodia, and displayed intricate carvings that highlighted the deeds of Khmer kings.

Large and small Buddhist statues peek out from the Pak Ou Caves of northern Laos. Spreading from Thailand, Theravada Buddhism took hold in Laos in the 1100s. By the 1300s, it was the official religion of the Lan Xang kingdom, the Lao realm set up by Prince Fa Ngum.

The Buddhist shrine That Dam, also known as the Black Stupa, dates from the early days of the Lan Xang kingdom.

an event that prompted a new wave of refugees to move into the fertile lands of the Mekong River.

Fa Ngum

Rivalry between the Tai people of Luang Prabang and the Khmer people of Kambuja led to the first unified state in Laos. In the fourteenth century, Fa Ngum, a Tai prince who had grown up in the imperial courts of Angkor, married the daughter of Jayavarman Paramesvara, the king of Kambuja. Seeing an opportunity to expand his power, Jayavarman then supplied Fa Ngum with an army and sent them northward to conquer Luang Prabang, which fell in 1353.

The army's success allowed Fa Ngum to found the kingdom of Lan Xang (Million Elephants in the Lao language). He expanded Lan Xang to include the lowlands east of the Mekong River and the plains of what is now northeastern Thailand. Fa Ngum decreed that Theravada Buddhism would be the official religion of his realm.

Under his orders, a mission sent to Angkor brought back a golden statue of the Buddha called the Prabang. Said to have magical powers, the Prabang would become a sacred symbol of the Laotian state and moved with the royal court whenever it changed locations.

Fa Ngum's son, Sam Sen Thai, succeeded to the throne of Lan Xang in 1373. A devout Buddhist, Sam Sen Thai oversaw the building of Buddhist wats throughout the kingdom. He further expanded Lan Xang and recruited a powerful standing army of 150,000 foot soldiers, horsemen, and elephant drivers. At the same time, Kambuja experienced decline and was overrun by Siam (modern Thailand). As Lan Xang continued to grow, it began to rival Siam and Burma, the two other major states in Southeast Asia.

Photo © John Elk III

A statue of King Setthathirath presides over the grounds of the Pha That Luang in Vientiane. This sixteenth-century ruler built the temple on the site of Khmer ruins soon after moving the royal court from Luang Prabang. Every November the compound hosts one of the country's major religious festivals.

Regional Rivalries

Never as powerful as its larger neighbors, Lan Xang suffered frequent attacks by Siamese and Burmese armies. By the 1500s, the Lan Xang king Setthathirath was fighting both the Burmese and the Khmer. To protect his territory, the king moved his capital from Luang Prabang to Vientiane, a location more central to Lao territories and easier to defend against Burmese attack. The Burmese invaded Lan Xang anyway in 1563 and occupied it for two years. In 1571, during a battle, Setthathirath mysteriously disappeared into the highlands of Laos.

Without a strong leader, Lan Xang was open to further attack. The Burmese soon conquered the kingdom and made it a vassal state (one that pays tribute to a stronger power). A succession of Burmese rulers, as well as Laotian allies of Burma, took power in Lan Xang. Meanwhile, conflict over the succession to the throne of Lan Xang prompted invasions. The armies of Siam and of Vietnam—which had overrun Champa by this time to become a power in the region—staked their claims to the land. For 20 years, Laos experienced nearly constant warfare.

This chaotic period ended in 1591 with the accession of Nokeo Koumane as the king of Lan Xang. By 1603 this monarch was no longer paying tribute to Burma and had reestablished Lan Xang as an independent state. Nevertheless, the internal struggles over the succession to the throne continued for many years. The conflicts ended in 1637, when the Lao king Souligna Vongsa seized power.

The Golden Age

A strong ruler, Souligna Vongsa expanded and defined the borders of Lan Xang and managed to live at peace with the Burmese and the Vietnamese. He built new monuments in Vientiane and was known for his support of Buddhism and of the arts.

A young girl performs the graceful movements of *lamvong* dancing. The reign of King Souligna Vongsa (1633–1690) saw a flowering of Lao culture and arts.

During Souligna Vongsa's reign, which Laotians consider the golden age of their history, European trading companies first arrived on the shores of Southeast Asia. The traders wanted to buy Asian goods to bring home to Europe. For example, Gerrit van Wuysthoff, an agent of a wealthy commercial firm called the Dutch East India Company, visited the Laotian capital in 1641. Soon afterward a Roman Catholic missionary from Italy, Giovanni Maria Leria, sought converts to his faith in Souligna Vongsa's territory.

The death of Souligna Vongsa in 1694 brought about another serious succession crisis that would eventually lead to the downfall of Lan Xang. Souligna Vongsa's two grandsons—one of them a young man called Kitsarat—were next in line to be ruler. But their youth and inexperience prompted ministers to fight over the throne.

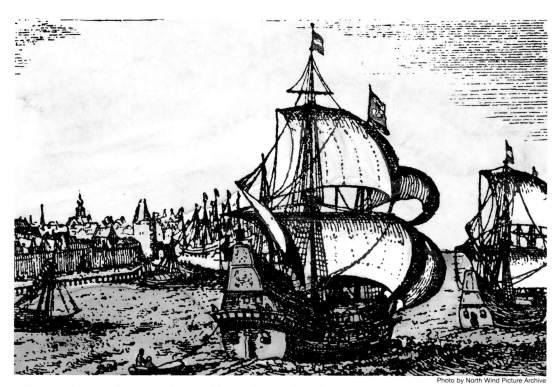

In the 1600s, Dutch trading ships left their home port of Amsterdam to seek new markets in Asia. A vessel from the Dutch East India Company dropped anchor long enough to send an agent to visit Vientiane in 1641.

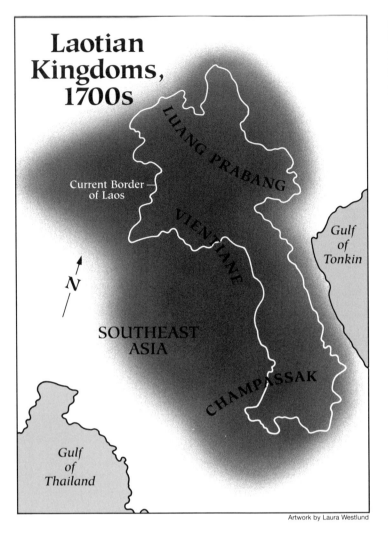

Laotian Kingdoms, 1700s

Current Border of Laos

N

SOUTHEAST ASIA

LUANG PRABANG

VIENTIANE

CHAMPASSAK

Gulf of Tonkin

Gulf of Thailand

Quarrels over the succession to the Lao throne caused the region to become divided into three separate realms—Luang Prabang in the north, Vientiane in central Laos, and Champassak in the south.

Artwork by Laura Westlund

At the same time, Sai Ong Hue, a nephew of Souligna Vongsa, asked the Vietnamese to help him win the crown. In exchange Sai Ong Hue would allow the Vietnamese to make Lan Xang a vassal state. In 1700, at the head of a Vietnamese army, Sai Ong Hue captured Vientiane.

Division and Decline

The new king forced Kitsarat to flee Laos. Kitsarat soon returned, seizing Luang Prabang and proclaiming himself king of northern Laos. Meanwhile, another relative established a kingdom of his own alongside the Mekong in Champassak. The result was the division of Laos into three kingdoms named after their capitals— Luang Prabang in the north, Vientiane in the center, and Champassak in the south.

For the next century, the three states suffered constant infighting as well as conflict with the kingdoms of Siam, Burma, and Vietnam. The political turmoil inspired Burma to invade in the mid-1700s. Within a few years, the Siamese—seeking to protect themselves against a Burmese invasion from Laos— overran Vientiane. To symbolize Siam's new dominance in the region, the Siamese captured the Prabang statue and took it to Bangkok, the Siamese capital.

By 1782 both Vientiane and Luang Prabang were vassals of Siam, which also had strong influence in Champassak. Siamese governors ruled over the Laotian states, and the Siamese also had the right to name the Laotian kings. Chou Anou, whom the Siamese chose as the king of Vientiane in 1805, served Siam as a military commander before his accession. But, after becoming king, he grew increasingly defiant of Siamese authority. In 1827 Chou Anou led an expedition against Bangkok. The campaign failed, the Laotian army was destroyed, and Siam took revenge by demolishing Vientiane. For the rest of the century, the former kingdom of Vientiane would be a province of Siam.

Colonial Laos

While the Laotian states were in turmoil, another foreign power came on the scene. Searching for a river route to China, French explorers and traders traveled up the wide Mekong River in the mid-1800s. France annexed (took over) southern Vietnam and Cambodia in the 1860s, hoping that the Mekong would be a dependable way to reach China's inland riches. France's dreams were dashed just north of the modern Laotian-Cambodian border, where the river passes through several miles of rocky falls and steep curves. Traveling farther upriver was impossible for large boats—the kind that transport trading goods.

Wat Si Saket in Vientiane dates from the early 1800s, when much of Laos was dominated by Siam (modern Thailand). Built by the Siamese-approved Lao king Chou Anou, the wat has a distinctly Siamese look. When Chou Anou rebelled in 1827, Siamese troops demolished much of the capital. The wat, perhaps because of its appearance, was spared destruction.

Photo © John Elk III

The remainder of Vietnam came under French rule in 1884. Three years later, the Laotian kingdoms experienced a similar fate. French diplomats signed an agreement with Siam to appoint a French official who would operate from the city of Vientiane. The Laotian monarch situated there held onto his throne but exercised little power or authority.

By 1893 France had claimed much of Southeast Asia—including Vietnam, Cambodia, and the three Laotian kingdoms—as French Indochina. The Laotian area was valued because it served as a mountainous borderland between French Indochina and Siam and Burma. These two Asian realms had links with Britain, France's European rival. In 1899 the French united the Laotian territories into a single entity known as Laos and recognized Sisavang Vong as the country's crown prince. (He assumed the throne several years later, upon returning to Laos from schooling abroad.)

Photo by Harlingue-Viollet

The French approved the appointment of Sisavang Vong as ruler of the united Laotian kingdom but allowed the king little power.

But Laos was considered only a minor part of French Indochina. Compared to Vietnam, which had more economic potential and drew many French colonists, few French people settled in Laos. The tiny, landlocked colony remained poor, underdeveloped, and geographically isolated. Those who did move to Laos were government officials and teachers.

Although a small class of French-educated Laotians rose, French or Vietnamese officials administered the colony with no help from the native population. Because of the remoteness of the country, its sparse population, and a general attitude of acceptance to foreign involvement, the Laotians escaped the harsh rule that French administrators were practicing in Vietnam.

Photo © Nevada Wier

By the late 1800s, Laos—as well as Vietnam and Cambodia—were under the control of France. French officials and diplomats in Vientiane and Luang Prabang began building European-style houses and mansions.

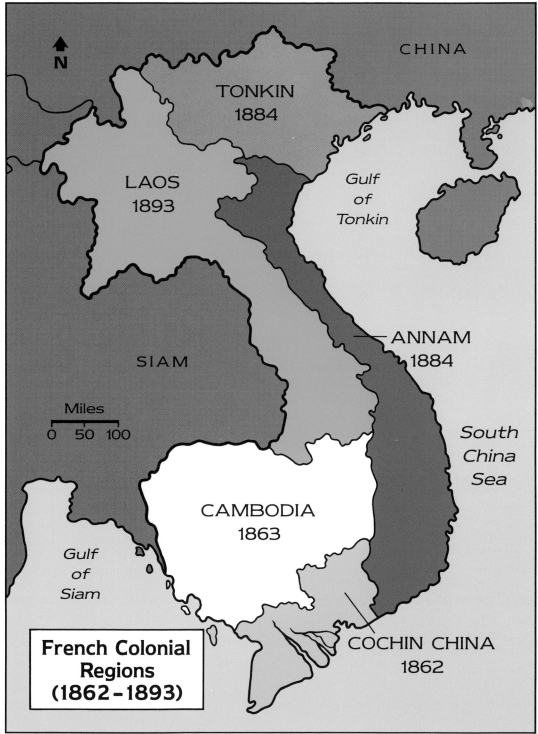

French Colonial Regions (1862–1893)

CHINA

N

TONKIN
1884

LAOS
1893

Gulf
of
Tonkin

SIAM

ANNAM
1884

Miles
0 50 100

South
China
Sea

CAMBODIA
1863

Gulf
of
Siam

COCHIN CHINA
1862

Artwork by Laura Westlund

Throughout the 1800s, France extended its influence in Southeast Asia. Treaties and attacks eventually gave the French authority over most of the region, beginning with southern Vietnam (Cochin China) in 1862. Laos was the last area added to what came to be called French Indochina.

In the mid-1940s, Laotians worked through various organizations to secure self-rule for their homeland. Some Laotians formed the revolutionary Free Laos Front and joined with a similar group—the Communist Viet Minh—to win independence for all of French Indochina. By 1949 the front's military arm, known as the Pathet Lao, was training its guerrilla forces.

The colonial regime in Laos changed during World War II (1939–1945), when Japanese soldiers overwhelmed the French forces and took control of much of Southeast Asia. Laos was spared most of the fighting, however, because the Japanese sailed around Indochina instead of marching through it.

After the defeat of Japan in 1945, the French returned to Indochina. But throughout the war, the people of Southeast Asia had developed a strong interest in governing themselves. Rather than be ruled by foreigners, Prince Phetsarath—the son of King Sisavang Vong—fled the country. He and others seeking Laotian independence started a movement in Thailand (formerly Siam) to free Laos from French rule.

In Vietnam, meanwhile, a guerrilla force known as the Viet Minh carried on their fight against French soldiers. The Viet Minh opposed French occupation as well as the monarchy, favoring a Communist government in which the state would own all property and would strictly control the economy. The various movements for self-rule in Southeast Asia worried the French.

Independence and Civil War

To calm anticolonial sentiments, the French wrote a constitution for Laos in 1947. They claimed the document would make Laos independent. But the government in exile, led by Prince Phetsarath, believed otherwise. To spearhead the drive to end colonialism in Laos, the prince recruited his brother Prince Souvanna Phouma and his half brother, Prince Souphanouvong.

In 1949 the exiled government, known as Lao Issara (Free Laos), expelled Souphanouvong for his support of the Communist Viet Minh. Souphanouvong then traveled to northern Vietnam, where he joined the Viet Minh and proclaimed the Democratic Republic of Laos. This declaration also helped to create a revolutionary military organization in Laos—similar to the Viet Minh—known as the Pathet Lao. At the same time, Souvanna Phouma dissolved the government in exile and returned to Laos to join a new royal regime, which had been established in accord with the French.

Overwhelmed by its ongoing war with Vietnam, France eventually agreed to give Laos complete independence in 1953. That same year, with the support of Viet Minh troops, Prince Souphanouvong opened a Pathet Lao headquarters in northeastern Laos. The assistance of the Communist government of North Vietnam would continue to be important throughout the course of Laos's Communist struggle.

In 1954 Vietnam defeated the French. At a postwar conference held in Geneva, Switzerland, France formally recognized the independence of all its former Indochinese colonies. The settlement gave the Pathet Lao control over two northern provinces. French-backed Laotian soldiers occupied the rest of Laos.

In the early 1950s, supported by the Viet Minh, Prince Souphanouvong led Pathet Lao troops into the jungles of Laos. His royal background and his willingness to be an active member of the revolution gave the movement legitimacy. In addition, Souphanouvong's early ties to the Viet Minh laid the foundation of Laos's long-standing connection to the Communist government of Vietnam.

The year after France withdrew from French Indochina, the Kingdom of Laos joined the United Nations and was recognized as an independent state within the international community. In spite of its newfound independence, however, Laos began to encounter serious internal political strife that would divide the country for the next 20 years.

When legislative elections took place in 1955, for example, the Pathet Lao refused to participate. They reasoned that the royalists did not have authority to call for elections in the northern provinces. When Prince Souvanna Phouma became the prime minister of the new Laotian government in 1956, Prince Souphanouvong stayed in northern Laos with the Communist forces.

ANTI-COMMUNIST ACTIVITIES

Negotiations eventually established a coalition leadership, bringing Souphanouvong into the government of the Kingdom of Laos. Elections in 1958 for the 21 assembly seats of the northern provinces resulted in 13 wins by the Pathet Lao's

political party, the Lao Patriotic Front. The United States, which was strongly anti-Communist, was unhappy with the election results and threatened to cut aid to Laos. To satisfy U.S. concerns, conservative Laotians in the coalition government arrested Souphanouvong and other Communist leaders. (They later escaped.)

To further oppose Communist influence, a faction of Laotian leaders formed the U.S.-backed, anti-Communist Committee for the Defense of National Interests. In response, the Communist governments in the Soviet Union and in North Vietnam gave the Pathet Lao aid. As political conflict worsened, the entire Laotian government collapsed in 1958. It was replaced by a new anti-Communist regime, headed by Phoui Sananikone, that refused to deal with the Pathet Lao. As with many of Laos's leaders during this turbulent era, his time in power was brief.

The continuing disagreement between the Laotian Communists and their opponents caused fighting to break out between royalist, Communist, and neutralist factions. (The less-powerful neutralists

While the Pathet Lao and Viet Minh were operating in northern Laos, a new government was taking shape in Vientiane. In 1959, in the presence of his court, King Savang Vatthana swore to uphold the Laotian constitution. A figurehead ruler, the king weathered more than 15 years of invasions, counterattacks, government reshuffles, and broken negotiations. In late 1975, when the Pathet Lao took over Laos, Savang Vatthana resigned. By 1977 he and his family were among 30,000 Laotians sent to prison for political crimes. Another 40,000 citizens were sent to reeducation camps to forcibly learn Communist doctrines.

favored neither side but wanted to bring about long-term political stability.)

The ongoing conflict also resulted in a complicated series of short-term governments. In mid-1960, a neutralist military group led by Kong Le, a young soldier who had grown tired of the fighting, took control of Vientiane and set up a new government. Six months later, Kong was overthrown by General Phoumi Nosavan, who installed his anti-Communist ally Boun Oum as prime minister. Phoumi was armed by foreign powers, such as the United States and Thailand, who wanted to limit Communist influence in Southeast Asia. At the same time, the Soviet Union and North Vietnam continued to supply the Pathet Lao.

Gains by the Communists

Phoumi's victory prompted the Pathet Lao to attack from their bases in northern Laos. In May 1961, the United States joined the Soviet Union and others in negotiating a cease-fire. In Geneva all sides agreed to a neutralist Government of National Unity under Souvanna Phouma.

The cease-fire lasted until April 1963, when the murder of a government minister renewed the fighting. During the next phase of the war, which lasted more than a decade, Souvanna Phouma struggled to run the country with members of the old neutralist administration.

From 1964 to 1973, conflicts erupted throughout Southeast Asia, especially in Vietnam, where the United States was heavily involved. The United States had air bases in Thailand, and U.S. planes frequently passed over Laos during bombing missions to Vietnam. Secret bombing of Pathet Lao regions was also common. In addition, the United States trained and supplied an army of nearly 10,000 Hmong soldiers for battle against the Pathet Lao forces.

Throughout the course of the Vietnam War, Laotian officials firmly believed that

Photo by Archive Photos/AFP

Laotian women were influential in the ranks of the Pathet Lao. Here, members prepare their weapons for inspection at a victory rally in the capital.

the outcome of the war would decide their future. If the Communists were successful in Vietnam and Cambodia, Laos would be bordered by three Communist nations—China, Vietnam, and Cambodia. Laotian politicians decided to prepare as best they could for a volatile future.

The Souvanna Phouma government opened negotiations with the Pathet Lao in 1972. In early 1973, as the United States was pulling out of the region, the two sides agreed to a cease-fire. Several coalition governments tried without success to run the country, and fighting continued in Laos between royalist soldiers and the Pathet Lao.

When the Communist movements in Vietnam and Cambodia were victorious in 1975, anti-Communist Laotians fled to Thailand. The Pathet Lao took control of Vientiane in August 1975, in a surprisingly bloodless finish to what had been a long and bloody war.

33

The Unknown Soldiers' Memorial in Vientiane honors Pathet Lao troops who died during Laos's civil war.

Photo © John Elk III

The Lao People's Democratic Republic

In December 1975, the new leaders declared the founding of the Lao People's Democratic Republic (LPDR). The new government allied with the Soviet Union and with China, two powerful Communist nations that had supported the Communist efforts in Southeast Asia. To enforce the change in power, the Pathet Lao cut most communications with the outside world and sent former government officials and members of the royalist army to work camps. At the camps, inmates were forced to learn Communist philosophy.

Prince Souphanouvong, the staunch supporter of the Pathet Lao, became the new president. He and other LPDR leaders, who had long been aligned with the Communist government of Vietnam, allowed thousands of Vietnamese troops to come inside Laos. Because Vietnam and China were not on good terms, the presence of Vietnamese forces made relations with China difficult. China quickly withdrew technicians who had been sent to aid the Laotians. Laos continued to receive help from the Soviet Union, however, and from the Soviet Union's allies in eastern Europe.

Photo © Andrew E. Beswick

A cyclist pedals in front of billboards that reflect Laos's Communist ties, especially to the former Soviet Union.

The postwar economic situation in Laos was bleak. Laos lost all aid from the United States, which had supported the anti-Communists. The LPDR took over private businesses and combined small farms into huge agricultural collectives. Economic assistance from fellow Communist countries increased, but the Laotian economy remained weak, dependent on foreign aid, and dominated by farming.

The government of the Lao People's Democratic Republic (LPDR) adopted Laos's national flag in 1975. It had long been the emblem of the Pathet Lao. Red represents the blood shed to win independence, and blue stands for the people's well-being. The white disk, which looks like a full moon, is an age-old Laotian symbol of happiness.

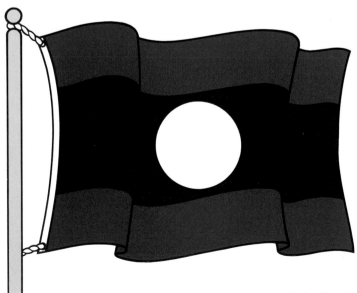

Artwork by Laura Westlund

35

Photo by AP/Wide World

The Hmong general Vang Pao was recruited by the United States in the 1960s to lead a secret army that opposed the Laotian Communists. He fled to Thailand in 1975, after Pathet Lao and North Vietnamese troops defeated the Hmong armies. Although some Hmong continue the anti-LPDR campaign, they are not a significant threat to LPDR stability.

Photo © Nevada Wier

Economic reforms enacted in the 1980s and 1990s allow market vendors to set their own prices for goods rather than be restricted by government guidelines.

Recent Events

Alliances with Communist countries continued to benefit Laos throughout the 1980s. But the nation's economy was still unable to recover from the years of civil unrest. Younger Communists felt the need for change. Governmental reforms slowly replaced outdated Communist policies and allowed a national election to be held in 1988.

LPDR leaders began to release political prisoners, such as the many Hmong citizens who had fought against the Pathet Lao during the war. These improvements were slowed by the continuing activities of a conservative political faction called the United Lao National Liberation Front. Headed by Outhong Souvannavong, the group claimed to have liberated large pieces of Laotian territory in the 1980s under the direction of the Hmong general Vang Pao. Government soldiers and General Vang's troops clashed.

Despite this conflict, the Lao People's Revolutionary party, the only legal political organization in Laos, went ahead with its plans to hold a congress (general meet-

ing) in 1991. The party's core group, the central committee, runs the party, which in turn runs the country.

During the congress, several veteran politicians retired, making half of the central committee members under 50 years of age. Earlier economic reforms were broadened, pushing the country away from a centralized system. The reforms inched Laos toward a free-market economy in which buyers and sellers determine what is sold and at what price.

The committee decided that economic reform should be one of the country's main goals and created a new constitution that permitted private ownership of property. This document was the country's first constitution since the LPDR took power in 1975. The new constitution enabled outside investors to own what they built or developed in Laos. Equally important were political reforms that reduced Vietnam's influence and its military personnel within Laos.

But the Laotian government still faces serious problems. Political and social reforms have been slower to develop than economic changes. Although Laos's constitution guarantees human rights, reports indicate that basic freedoms—such as speech, assembly, travel, privacy, and, to a degree, religion—are denied. In addition, political corruption and theft have drained the state of money and property.

Since the collapse of Soviet Communism in the early 1990s, Laos has concentrated on relations with other countries, particularly its Indochinese neighbors. While Laos welcomes such interaction, the small nation also worries about potential cultural domination from stronger, more developed lands such as Thailand. Foreigners, on the other hand, are eager to invest money in Laos. If government leaders can make progress in addressing Laos's internal needs, the country may yet be able to slow economic and social decline.

Government

According to the 1991 constitution, the highest-ranking government official in Laos is the president, who is appointed for a five-year term by the National Assembly, the country's legislature. The president names a prime minister and the members of the Council of Ministers—a group that directs the operations of the government's various ministries.

Legislative power belongs to the 85 elected members of the National Assembly. Adult males and females over the age of 18 elect these officials for a period of five years. The Lao People's Revolutionary party continues to be the only legal political party, and those who wish to run for office must be party members. On the local level, governors chosen by the president run the nation's 17 provinces.

Laos's judicial system includes the Supreme People's Court, the nation's highest court, whose members are named by the National Assembly. The legislature also appoints the judges of provincial and municipal courts. District and military courts operate with limited jurisdiction (authority to apply the law).

The head of the Laotian government is the president, who resides in a colonial-style estate at one end of Lan Xang Street in Vientiane. In 1996 the president was Nouhak Phoumsavan, an old-time revolutionary who had been in the jungles with Prince Souphanouvong in the 1950s. Nouhak named Khamtai Siphandon, the leader of the Laotian People's Revolutionary party, to be the nation's prime minister.

Piles of freshly harvested produce and consumer goods crowd a market stall in the capital's Khua Din market.

3) The People

Laos remains a largely rural nation. Only about 19 percent of its 4.8 million people live in cities. Laos has about 54 persons per square mile, making the country one of the most sparsely populated nations in all of Asia. More than half the Laotians are lowlanders who make a living as farmers. The rivers that provide irrigation for rice growing run through narrow east-west valleys, keeping the people isolated from one another. As a result, languages and customs may differ from one valley to the next. Isolated living conditions are common for mountain-dwelling people as well.

The population of Laos is young—around 45 percent of the people are less than 15 years of age. The number of Laotians is also growing rapidly, the result of a high birthrate that is partly due to the government's ban on birth-control devices. At the annual growth rate of 2.8 percent, the country's population will double in 25 years.

Ethnic Groups

Laos has as many as 68 ethnic groups living within its borders. About two-thirds of this diverse population are ethnic Lao-Lum—often more simply referred to as Lao—who mostly dwell in the country's lowlands. Other significantly large groups include the Lao-Tai (Tai), Lao-Theung (also known as Mon-Khmer), and the Lao-Soung (including the Hmong and the Mien peoples).

A lake gives a lowland village *(left)* a place to anchor small boats. Almost half of the Laotian population, such as these girls in Luang Prabang *(bottom left),* are younger than 15. Traditional headgear *(bottom right)* distinguishes this man as a member of the Lao-Theung, one of the nation's larger ethnic groups.

Photo © John Elk III

Photo © Nevada Wier

Photo © Brian Vikander

Laotian hill people have their own languages and traditions that are distinct from those of the lowland groups. The hill people may be Hmong, Mien, Tai (also spelled Thai), or any of dozens of offshoots from larger groups. Among the Tai hill dwellers, the color of clothing worn by adult females identifies the group. For example, a person is a Black Tai or a Red Tai, as suggested by the traditional color the women of the village wear.

Although hill people trade with their Lao neighbors, relations between the two groups can be strained. The Hmong, for example, fought against Communism during the war and have since suffered at the hands of Laos's Communist government. Many have departed their highland retreats, crossing the wide Mekong River into Thailand. As of the mid-1990s, 20 years after the end of the war, thousands of Laotian citizens remain in refugee camps within Thailand, while many others have moved to the United States.

Photo by UPI/Bettmann

In the late 1970s, many ethnic minorities, including these boys from the Yao group (above), **fled Laos for refugee camps in Thailand. By the 1990s, some of the refugees were returning** (below).

Photo by J.M. Micaud/United Nations High Commissioner for Refugees

Yao villagers build their dwellings on stilts to protect them from flooding during the rainy season.

A husband and wife work together to set up a bamboo fence around their house. Bamboo is one of the more common woods used in home construction in Laos.

Village and Family Life

Traditions vary among Laotians, depending on where they are located and how they make a living. The two main population groupings are the lowlanders, who farm in the Mekong River Valley, and the hill people, who move from place to place in isolated, mountainous areas.

LOWLANDERS

A typical Laotian farm family lives in a village with fewer than 2,500 residents. Laotian households are large and often include three generations. As the household grows, the family adds new rooms to accommodate its members. The people build their houses on stilts—a precaution against flooding caused by monsoon rains.

Food preparation in lowland villages sometimes takes place in the shade beneath the house, where pigs and chickens may be penned. The shaded area may also be used by family members as they weave clothing or repair farm equipment.

41

Almost every Laotian village has a Buddhist pagoda (temple) and at least one monk who is in charge of religious needs and schooling. Whether a nonreligious schoolmaster or a monk, the teacher faces crowded classes with few facilities.

As important as the monk is the village headman. (By tradition monks and civic leaders are men.) The headman may inherit his position or win it through an election. He decides various local matters, ranging from resolving a disagreement between two neighbors to designing and locating the village gate. His authority in the village is absolute. Tradition dictates that not even the president of the country can overrule a headman within the boundaries of his own village.

An open marketplace serves as the central meeting place in most villages. Here farmers sell everything from pigs to fruit and tobacco. Shoppers may also find necessities such as batteries, combs, and clothing. The marketplace is open every day in larger towns. In a smaller village, the market may be a weekly event. Farm families grow most of what they eat and sell their surplus in the market or to rice exporters.

Success for a farming family depends on the rice harvest. Early every morning, families eat a quick meal and then walk or ride an animal or a small plow to their rice paddy. They work until about noon, then go home for a meal. After resting during the hottest part of the day, they return to the paddies to work until almost dark. During the growing season, this schedule is observed daily throughout Southeast Asia.

Photo © Nevada Wier

Buddhist monks traditionally guided the affairs of most Laotian villages.

The weekly or daily market gives neighbors an opportunity to visit and to buy necessities they cannot make themselves.

Photo © Nevada Wier

HILL PEOPLE

Most hill people in Laos practice slash-and-burn agriculture. To create cropland for rice, vegetables, fruits, and illegal opium poppies, they clear land by setting trees and brush on fire. After a few seasons of growing crops on the burned-off ground, the hill people tend to move to other areas because the soil has become infertile and can no longer support plants.

The Hmong, who make up one of Laos's largest ethnic groups, mostly live in hard-to-reach areas. The LPDR has long suspected the Hmong of anti-Communist activities, a view that has resulted in clashes between the Hmong and government forces.

Photo © Nevada Wier

Photo © Tovya Wager/Asian Pacific Adventures

Photo © Brian Vikander

A boy *(left)* rides his family's water buffalo, while a member of the Ko people models a distinctive head covering *(right)*.

In recent years, the government has tried to stop slash-and-burn farming, which causes permanent deforestation of the Laotian countryside. But the new policy, which includes moving hill people onto level areas such as the historic Plain of Jars, has been only partially effective. Forced moves have made the hill people suspicious of the government, which also has been unable to control the production of opium poppies.

Many hill people are nomadic, so attempts to make them stay in one place are difficult. The hill farmers prefer to search for new locations between one growing season and the next. One result of such a lifestyle is that very few hill-dwelling children settle into a school long enough to learn to read and write.

Language and Education

There are three major languages spoken in Laos. Most lowlanders speak Lao, the nation's official tongue, which is close to the language spoken in Thailand. Written Lao uses a modified form of the Sanskrit alphabet. The language itself is tonal—a one-syllable word can have very different meanings, depending on how it is pronounced. Lao Soung is spoken by the Hmong and the Mien. The Laotian Tai of the highlands have their own dialect, called Lao Theung, which is similar to Mon-Khmer, the language of Cambodia.

Careful listeners also may hear other languages throughout Laos. In Vientiane a small number of older Laotians use French. In contrast, Tibeto-Burman languages are common along the border with Myanmar and China. Thai, Chinese, and Vietnamese living in Laos use the languages of their home countries. English can be heard, primarily in business and government centers in Vientiane and along the Mekong River.

Education is compulsory for all children between the ages of seven and fifteen, but

The sign at a dentist's office in Luang Prabang displays written Lao, which is based on Sanskrit—an ancient Indian alphabet.

Elementary school students *(above)* **struggle to pay attention in Luang Prabang. Laotian boys** *(left)* **have traditionally had a better chance than Laotian girls of finishing their education.**

most students attend for an average of only six years. Lao is the language of instruction. Aware of a lack of school facilities, the government permitted the establishment of private schools in 1990. Only 50 percent of the population can read, and almost twice as many women as men are illiterate. Laotian families traditionally have felt it more important to educate sons than daughters. The government hopes to address this problem with privately operated schools.

Religion

The chief religion followed in Laos is Theravada Buddhism, but many Laotians also honor spirits, called *phi,* which guide the individual in daily life. These separate sets of religious beliefs are not necessarily in conflict. Many Laotians feel that Buddhism looks after the eternal soul, while the practice of honoring spirits—called animism—helps a person with more earthly problems. Animists believe that spirits inhabit rivers, forests, rocks, and many other natural features. These spirits may be appeased by the faithful who place small offerings of food, little flags, and incense in obvious places.

Buddhism began in India in the sixth century B.C. The faith traces its origins to Siddhartha Gautama, a prince who went on a prolonged search for the meaning of life. After gaining enlightenment, Gautama became known as the Buddha and

Photo © Nevada Wier

A small shrine honors *phi,* or spirits, which many Laotians believe influence daily life.

Photo © John Elk III

The altar at Wat Si Muang is among the most visited sacred spots in Laos. One of the statues of the Buddha is said to be able to grant wishes or to answer especially nagging questions. If a person's request has been heard, the worshiper is supposed to return bearing offerings of food, incense, and candles.

A mural in Vientiane *(above)* shows the Buddha teaching. Another image *(below)*—of the Buddha pushing away fear—stands in Wat Pha Keo, a museum located on the site of a royal temple.

won followers to his teachings in India. Buddhism became India's official religion, which early traders spread to Thailand and across Southeast Asia. In the fourteenth century A.D., King Fa Ngum declared Buddhism to be the official religion of Laos. Buddhist pagodas and monks became important features of Laotian life.

Laos is one of the few Communist nations in which Buddhists are allowed to continue practicing their faith. (Most Communist countries ban religion.) This openness to Buddhism may be because Buddhist teachings reject material wealth, a philosophy that does not conflict with Communist ideology. Regardless of the cause, Laotian Buddhists fared much better than their counterparts in Cambodia, where temples were burned and monks were systematically killed.

Ethnic Chinese and Vietnamese practice a blend of Buddhism and Chinese Confucianism. Roman Catholic and Protestant missionaries converted a few hill people to Christianity in the 1950s. A very small

Wat Xieng Khwan south of Vientiane is dubbed Buddha Park by locals because of the colossal statues of the Buddha and of Hindu gods. The grounds are the work of Luang Pu, a religious cult leader of the 1950s, whose beliefs mixed Buddhist and Hindu ideas.

portion of the Laotian population remains Christian. Since the Communist revolution of 1975, the government has not allowed religious missionary work. Foreigners trying to convert Laotians have been fined and ordered out of the country.

Health

Tropical diseases continue to challenge the Laotian medical system. The infant mortality rate (the number of babies who die within their first year) is 98 in every 1,000 live births. This number is quite high for

A Laotian doctor speaks about childhood immunization at a clinic in the capital. The country's doctor-patient ratio is about 1 to 6,500.

Northern Laos has long been an area for growing opium poppies, from which the illegal drug heroin can be made. Bad weather in the early 1990s destroyed much of the crop, which now is estimated only to meet domestic needs. (Estimated percentages of the crop by northern province from the U.S. Drug Enforcement Agency's *National Narcotics Intelligence Consumers Committee Report,* 1994.)

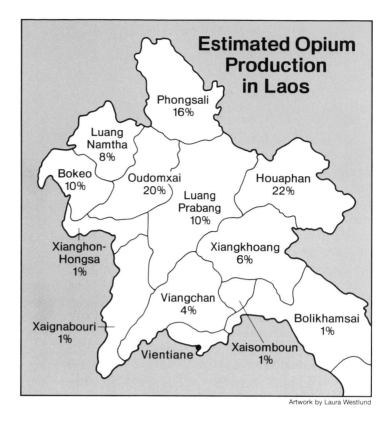

Estimated Opium Production in Laos

Phongsali 16%

Luang Namtha 8%

Bokeo 10%

Oudomxai 20%

Luang Prabang 10%

Houaphan 22%

Xianghon-Hongsa 1%

Xiangkhoang 6%

Viangchan 4%

Bolikhamsai 1%

Xaignabouri 1%

Xaisomboun 1%

Vientiane

Artwork by Laura Westlund

Southeast Asia, with only Cambodia exceeding Laos's rate. The life expectancy rate for Laotian citizens is 52 years, which is lower than the figure for most Southeast Asian countries.

Although infant mortality is going down, illnesses such as malaria and hemorrhagic fever are still problems. Other diseases— less serious but disabling if left untreated—include dysentery, hepatitis, and tuberculosis. No national immunization program exists, and the rice-based Laotian diet lacks proteins and minerals. Another health hazard, particularly among hill people and loggers, is injury and death from unexploded bombs and shells left from the war era.

Drug addiction is an additional health problem for the people of Laos. The country has an estimated 40,000 addicts, most of whom are opium smokers. With the help of the United Nations, Laos recently opened its first detoxification and reha-

bilitation center. Drug officials from Myanmar and Thailand have also agreed to work with Laos to stop drug use and production. To encourage farmers to stop growing opium poppies and to cultivate other crops, the government has begun rural development projects.

Because of a poor road system, transportation to hospitals and clinics is difficult. A recent study found 558 doctors, 2,346 medical workers, and 6,600 first-aid workers in the country. On average, only one hospital bed exists for every 369 persons in Laos, and only one physician is available to practice medicine for every 6,495 persons.

Festivals and the Arts

Buddhism has no regular religious services, but Laotians observe various holidays with festivals that center around the village pagoda. To celebrate the Buddha's birth, the Buddha's death, the Laotian New Year, and other dates, the people set off rockets and fireworks and enjoy music, food, and drink. These festive occasions provide opportunities for young, unmarried men and women from nearby villages to meet.

Orchestras have been a part of Laotian festivals for several centuries. Musical instruments include two-stringed violins with single-string bows, xylophones, drums, and lutes. More recently, Laotian musicians have also taken up accordions, banjos, and guitars. Recorded music heard on cassettes and on the radio is threatening the existence of live orchestras, which remain popular for weddings and festivals.

The graceful *lamvong* dance often accompanies the music. Known outside Asia as Thai-style dancing, lamvong is a folk dance in which participants move slowly in a large circle, often on or around a platform built especially for the occasion. Their hands slowly shoot imaginary arrows, play imaginary instruments, and beckon audiences.

Plays and puppet shows often use stories from the nation's most popular piece of literature, the *Ramayana,* as their inspiration. Originating in India, the home of the Sanskrit language, this Hindu epic poem tells of dashing heroes, vengeful gods, nasty demons, monkey armies, and more.

Traditional Lao flower arrangements brighten temples during Buddhist festivals.

The top of the Patuxai, a pre-revolutionary war memorial, features Lao-style artwork.

Laos has a strong craft tradition. The hill people of Laos produce striking jewelry and cloth. Metalsmiths hammer necklaces, earrings, bracelets, and other objects out of silver or pewter. Handwoven scarves are also worn by highlanders. Handmade rugs depict religious and spiritual scenes.

Pottery also has been a popular art form for centuries. Tiles, jars, plates, and teapots sized from tiny to quite large are

The sale to tourists of intricately woven textiles (above) **and brightly painted masks** (right) **brings foreign income into the country.**

seen all across Laos. Perhaps the most famous works of pottery are the ancient, huge containers that dot the Plain of Jars.

Craftspeople also produce lacquerware, usually bowls, trays, and other objects. Lacquer, once produced from the natural sap of the son tree, is now made artificially but still leaves a mirrorlike finish over painted wood. Gold, inlaid pearl, and other treasures adorn the finished pieces. Another widespread craft is the fashioning of the tiny metal Buddha figures that many Laotians carry or wear.

Food

Because most Laotian households have no refrigeration, people shop daily for fresh food at street markets. Laotians commonly eat water buffalo, pork, or chicken just hours after the slaughter. Also popular are prepared foods such as *foe* (rice noodle soup). Offered from a pushcart, this filling and nourishing dish includes steaming broth, noodles, bits of beef, coriander leaves, and slices of onion. Fruits popular among Laotians are bananas, guavas, papayas, pineapples, plums, and many forms of citrus, such as grapefruits, lemons, limes, and oranges.

Laotians also dine on freshwater fish, strong-smelling fish sauce, chilies that range from mild to very hot, a variety of vegetables, and rice. Cooks serve either rice or noodles with virtually every meal. The rice is sticky enough to be rolled into a small ball and eaten with the hands. French-style bread is available in Vientiane and other large cities, where a European breakfast of a roll, jam, and coffee is gaining popularity.

Laos has one brewery, which distributes its products to major cities within the country. There are also several soft drinks on the market. One of the most popular beverages is sugarcane juice, which vendors often prepare fresh on street corners. Other drinks favored by Laotians are soybean milk, coconut milk, fruit juice, coffee, and tea. The latter two beverages are locally grown and often drunk hot with milk and sugar.

Photo © Andrew E. Beswick

Vendors at a food stall offer traditional dishes to passersby.

Although not for everyone, roasted insects tempt some Laotian diners.

Photo © Nevada Wier

Much of Laos's manufacturing output—especially of soft drinks, soap powder, and processed food—remains in the country to satisfy local demands. Imported goods mainly come from Thailand.

4) The Economy

After Laos's civil war ended in 1975, the country faced serious economic problems. One of the poorest nations in Southeast Asia, Laos had a low standard of living, with most families continuing to produce only enough food to feed the members. This form of agriculture, called subsistence farming, leaves no surplus crops to sell at local markets.

With most people involved in agriculture, little opportunity existed to develop other sectors of the economy. In addition, the government's Communist policies—including state (rather than private) ownership of businesses—slowed foreign investment. The outside income was desperately needed to build and modernize the country's industries. Furthermore, because it was aligned with Vietnam, Laos

suffered poor relations with its more powerful neighbors—Thailand and China.

During its early years among the world's Communist nations, Laos got economic aid chiefly from the Soviet Union and from Vietnam. Laotian leaders realized, however, that they could not depend on outsiders for their country's well-being in the long run. By 1980 reformers had introduced some new policies that relaxed the tight controls the state had placed on the economy.

The government loosened its ban on private ownership in 1986. Soon afterward small, privately owned stores began to open, first in Vientiane and then in other cities. In 1988 foreign investment in Laos again became legal. By the mid-1990s, foreign enterprises were springing up throughout Laos, where labor is cheap and plentiful. A real-estate boom has since taken place in and around Vientiane.

Agriculture and Forestry

Wood and agricultural products make up more than half the Laotian gross national product (GNP)—the total value of all goods and services produced in a year. Although timber and sawn wood account for almost 40 percent of all exports, Laos sells few of its fruits, vegetables, or grains abroad. In fact, food production remains an ongoing problem, with imports of food still outpacing exports.

To feed its people, Laos depends heavily on its annual harvest of rice, which occupies 85 percent of all cultivated land. But when droughts, floods, and pests cause poor harvests, reports of malnutrition are common. The country must sometimes accept foreign food aid, even to supply provinces that usually have surplus crops.

Laotian farmers also grow corn, cassavas, potatoes, sweet potatoes, cotton, tobacco, and coffee. Typical livestock includes pigs, buffalo, poultry, and cattle, with pigs being the most common farm animal. Aquaculture (fish farming) is also an important agricultural activity. About half of all farming is done on state-run cooperatives, where growers share the work and the income from harvests. Private farms account for the other half of agricultural production.

An important challenge facing Laos is the poor management of its forest resources. In 1989 forests covered 40 percent of all land—yet deforestation was increasing. In the same year, the government banned the export of unprocessed timber and in 1991 passed legislation to stop uncontrolled logging. Despite these measures, wood products remain one of the country's principal exports.

The government is also dealing with the harvest of opium poppies, which—when processed—contain the illegal drug heroin.

Photo © Nigel Sitwell/The Hutchison Library

Workers plant rice seedlings in a flooded field, or paddy, near the Mekong River.

Photo © Luke Golobitsh

Lumber from Laos's vast woodlands awaits transport.

In remote valleys near the borders with Myanmar and China, Laotian villagers grow poppies, cutting the buds and collecting the sap for sale to heroin processors. Laws in Laos ban the growing of poppies, but the government does little to enforce the regulations. As a result, northern Laos—a part of the so-called Golden Triangle—has become a major source of the world's heroin.

Energy and Mining

The generation of hydroelectricity has become one of the most important economic activities in Laos. By the year 2000, the government plans to produce more than five times the electricity created by river dams, even though present output exceeds Laotian needs. Laos sells its surplus electricity to its more industrialized neighbors—such as Thailand—who cannot generate power as cheaply. While the hydroelectric industry offers real growth for the Laotian economy, conservationists fear that unchecked development will have a harmful effect on the natural environment.

Although the Laotian government controls most power-producing facilities, the private sector also is involved. Five different companies are working on the Nam Theun Dam, which will cost about $1 billion by its completion in the late 1990s. Along with Thailand, Australia is aiding Laos in the design and construction of new hydroelectric projects.

Laos does not need a large supply of petroleum because hydroelectricity is readily available and because the country has so few gas-fueled vehicles. The country imports most of its gasoline and diesel fuel from Brunei, a small oil-exporting nation on the Asian island of Borneo. Most Laotian homes use wood charcoal for cooking and heating.

Tin and gypsum are the two most commonly mined minerals, with more than 110 tons of tin and 124 tons of gypsum extracted each year. Although Laos has coal deposits, most are located in remote areas and remain undeveloped.

A Laotian work crew labors on one of the country's dams, the largest of which is the Nam Ngun facility near the capital. The sale of hydroelectric power to neighboring nations may be a means of strengthening Laos's economy in the future.

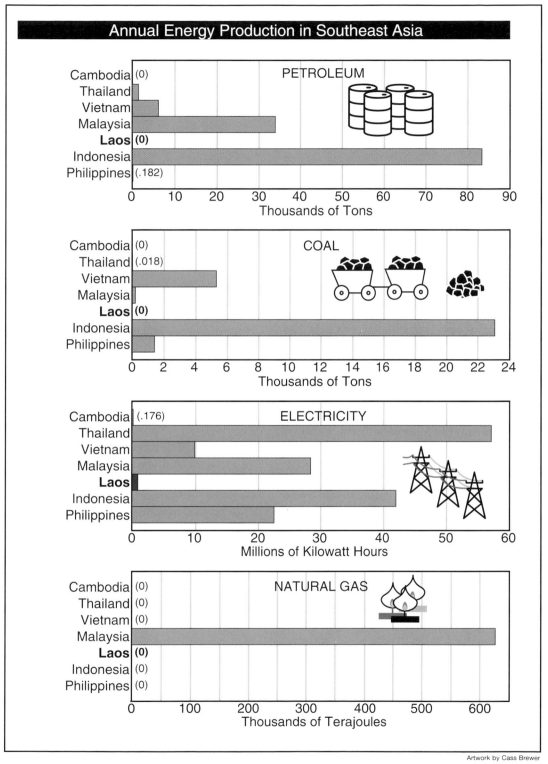

Annual Energy Production in Southeast Asia

PETROLEUM

Cambodia (0)
Thailand
Vietnam
Malaysia
Laos (0)
Indonesia
Philippines (.182)

Thousands of Tons
(0, 10, 20, 30, 40, 50, 60, 70, 80, 90)

COAL

Cambodia (0)
Thailand (.018)
Vietnam
Malaysia
Laos (0)
Indonesia
Philippines

Thousands of Tons
(0, 2, 4, 6, 8, 10, 12, 14, 16, 18, 20, 22, 24)

ELECTRICITY

Cambodia (.176)
Thailand
Vietnam
Malaysia
Laos
Indonesia
Philippines

Millions of Kilowatt Hours
(0, 10, 20, 30, 40, 50, 60)

NATURAL GAS

Cambodia (0)
Thailand (0)
Vietnam (0)
Malaysia
Laos (0)
Indonesia (0)
Philippines (0)

Thousands of Terajoules
(0, 100, 200, 300, 400, 500, 600)

Artwork by Cass Brewer

This chart shows domestic energy production in various Southeast Asian countries in the 1990s. Virtually all of Laos's energy comes from hydroelectric power. (Data from *Key Indicators of Developing Asian and Pacific Countries*, 1994.)

Trucks loaded with valuable timber, one of Laos's main exports, begin their journey from Vientiane to Thailand.

Manufacturing and Trade

Factories employ 5 percent of the Laotian workforce. Important manufactured goods include tires, textiles, clothing, plastic products, animal feed, bricks, beer, soft drinks, and soap powder. Most of the foods and drinks produced in Laos are sold within the country, while tires are exported. The state continues to have a hand in industry, producing plywood in a large factory in Vientiane.

Thailand is by far the largest customer for Laotian goods, followed by France, Germany, and Japan. Laos's principal exports are timber and wood products, electricity, textiles and garments, coffee, tin, and gypsum. Despite a rise in exports, however, Laos still runs a trade deficit, meaning the country spends more on foreign goods than it receives for its exports. Thailand—the largest source of Laos's imports—supplies rice and many other consumer goods, ranging from electronics to vehicles, machinery, and construction equipment.

Japan, China, and Italy also sell goods to Laos.

Once closed to most foreign investment, Laos has passed laws making it easier for foreigners to invest or build in the country. After Thailand the leading investors in Laos are the United States, Australia, China, France, Hong Kong, and Taiwan. Laos has sold land for the construction of hotels, casinos, duty-free shops, and golf courses. The government receives about 200 applications a month from foreign groups seeking to construct everything from wood-production facilities to garment factories.

Free-trade reforms have also led to rapid development. To enhance this growth, the Laotian government has decided to join the Association of Southeast Asian Nations (ASEAN). Membership in this diplomatic and trading group may increase foreign investment in Laos. The ASEAN member Malaysia, for example, has a strong economy that would provide a ready market for Laotian products. Laos is already part of several ASEAN educational and technical projects.

Transportation

A landlocked nation, Laos has an inadequate transportation system. For example, the road between Vientiane and Luang Prabang often needs repair and can become rutted and narrow. During the long rainy season, the monsoons often flood the roads and disrupt traffic. Laos has no railway system and offers little public transportation of any kind between provinces. The Mekong River provides an important route for ferries and cargo boats, but navigation is treacherous during the dry season, when low water levels reveal dangerous boulders. Interior waterways are likewise hazardous and unpredictable.

Photo © Nevada Wier

Small businesses, such as family operated textile mills, provide consumer goods within Laos and attract earnings from tourists.

Laotians regularly use the country's river system, especially the Mekong, for transportation.

Photo © Nik Wheeler

Friendship Bridge crosses the Mekong to link Laos with Thailand, the source of most of Laos's imports and the destination of most of the nation's exports.

About 90 percent of all freight and 95 percent of all passenger traffic in Laos moves by road. Yet the country has less than 2,500 miles of main roads and about 3,500 miles of secondary roads.

In the early 1990s, Laos and Thailand cooperated on the construction of the Mittaphab (Friendship) Bridge. This project, which opened in 1994, is fostering a busy trade between the two countries. In the mid-1990s, the government laid plans for a second bridge across the Mekong, probably linking the Laotian town of Thakhek with Nakhon Phanom in northeastern Thailand. From there a road will run through Laos and across Vietnam, ending at a port on the South China Sea. The new route will help Thailand, Laos, and Vietnam ship their products overseas.

Laos has two commercial and two smaller airports. The nation's state-run airline, Lao Aviation, began operations in

Passengers leave a Lao Aviation flight that has just landed in Luang Prabang.

Visitors marvel at the huge containers strewn about the Plain of Jars. Historians disagree on the use and crafting of the jars, some of which weigh more than a ton. They may have stored rice or wine or perhaps been used as tombs. Some rock specialists think the jars are made of sandstone, while others speculate that they are of a unique type of cement.

1976 with flights between Vientiane and Luang Prabang. By the 1990s, the company was flying to and from Bangkok, the capital of Thailand, and Ho Chi Minh City (formerly Saigon), Vietnam. Thai Airlines and Singapore Airlines, as well as an occasional tour operator, fly into Vientiane.

Tourism

Once closed to foreigners, Laos now allows limited stays by travelers. All persons who want to visit Laos must apply for a visa through a Laotian embassy or consulate. Tourists either fly into Vientiane or travel overland, crossing from Thailand into Laos via the Mittaphab Bridge. Travelers who are not part of group tours may only visit the Vientiane area. For this reason, group tours account for most of the annual total of about 130,000 visitors.

One of the most popular stops for these tours is the Plain of Jars, where prehis-

toric settlers left the landscape strewn with large containers. Other attractions include the historic capital of Luang Prabang, tribal villages, Buddhist temples, ruins of Khmer cities, and the Pak Ou Caves along the Mekong. Visitors to the countryside enjoy Laotian music, local food, and traditional dances and crafts.

More and more tourists are traveling to the eastern edge of Laos for a glimpse at what once was the Ho Chi Minh Trail. Because Laos has no railways and only poor roads, this is a strenuous trip. But the hardy traveler can still view rusting Soviet and Chinese trucks along the once-hidden pathway that saw heavy bombing and fighting during the Vietnam War.

Tourism is helping the Laotian economy by bringing in foreign income. Yet the rising number of visitors is also putting a strain on the country's limited facilities. The government's challenge is to accommodate visitors while maintaining the

The trip to the Pak Ou Caves is by boat along the Mekong. Tourists usually hire a vessel in nearby Luang Prabang and arrange for the boat handlers to also stop at villages along the way.

Photo © John Elk III

Photo © John Elk III

The wall hangings, mosaics, carvings, statuary, and other works of Luang Prabang draw many travelers to the old capital. Considered one of the best-preserved examples of traditional Southeast Asian art and architecture, the compact city holds more than 30 historic wats and is located in an appealing setting.

kind of unspoiled and peaceful setting that most tourists seek.

The Future

Laotians are facing an uncertain future. For the first time in two centuries, the government of Laos is in the position to fully represent itself in the international realm. As the country struggles to make its mark, it must also juggle a variety of concerns.

Although foreign governments and citizens are seeking to invest in the country, many Laotians still suffer poverty and malnutrition. Laotian farmers are not always able to feed their families, and the average Laotian worker earns only the equivalent of $180 a year. A poorly trained workforce also puts Laos at a disadvantage in the competition for foreign investment. The government needs to prepare workers for new manufacturing and service jobs.

The historic rivalry and prejudice between lowland Laotians and people of the hills is also a continuing concern. Many of the Hmong, for example, were hunted down and killed for their support of U.S. operations in Laos during the war. Those who survived the conflict fled the country.

Rapid development and the expanding economy pose other dilemmas for the people of Laos. Although they seek a better way of life, they also fear the loss of their customs, traditions, and beliefs. Controlled development, with a concern for the environment and for maintaining Laotian culture, is the most important challenge to Laos as it enters the twenty-first century.

Photo by Andrew E. Beswick

Photo by Andrew E. Beswick

Girls in a river outside Vientiane strike a positive gesture *(top),* **while boys enjoy an after-school session of foosball** *(above).*

Index